I0628995

HOCKEY >>
SEASON TICKET

THE ULTIMATE FAN GUIDE

BY CHRIS PETERS

First Edition
First Printing, 2019

Book design by Sarah Taplin
Cover design by Sarah Taplin
Photographs ©: Robin Alam/Icon Sportswire/AP Images, cover (top); Alex Gor/ Shutterstock Images, cover (middle background); Jeanine Leech/Icon Sportswire/AP Images, cover (bottom left); Jeff Speer/Icon Sportswire/AP Images, cover (bottom right top); Graham Hughes/The Canadian Press /AP Images, cover (bottom right bottom); David Zalubowski/AP Images, 4; meunierd/Shutterstock Images, 8; Richard Drew/AP Images, 11, 43; ophotography/Shutterstock Images, 12; Darryl Dyck/The Canadian Press/AP Images, 16–17, 63; Daniel Lea/Cal Sport Media/AP Images, 19; AP Images, 20, 22–23, 33, 36, 41, 46, 54, 57, 60; Preston Stroup/AP Images, 26; Reed Saxon/AP Images, 28; Larry Macdougall/AP Images, 35; Gene J. Puskar/AP Images, 45; Ryan Remiorz/AP Images, 50; Julie Jacobson/AP Images, 53; David Duprey/AP Images, 64, 66–67; Elise Amendola/AP Images, 71; Fred Kfoury III/Icon Sportswire/AP Images, 72; Jim Mone/AP Images, 76; Paul Sancya/AP Images, 79; Peter Joneleit/Cal Sport Media/AP Images, 80; Nick Wass/AP Images, 83; Rusty Kennedy/ AP Images, 87; John Locher/AP Images, 88; Kathy Willens/AP Images, 91; Mike Wulf/Cal Sport Media/AP Images, 94–95; Red Line Editorial, 96–97

Design Elements ©: Shutterstock Images

Press Box Books, an imprint of Press Room Editions

Library of Congress Control Number: 2018940606

ISBN:
978-1-63494-037-5 (paperback)
978-1-63494-042-9 (epub)
978-1-63494-047-4 (hosted ebook)

Distributed by North Star Editions, Inc.
2297 Waters Drive
Mendota Heights, MN 55120
www.northstareditions.com

Printed in the United States of America

TABLE OF CONTENTS

CHAPTER 1

THE STANLEY CUP

The voice of ESPN announcer Gary Thorne boomed: "After 22 years: Raymond Bourque!"

As Thorne called the action, Colorado Avalanche captain Joe Sakic handed the Stanley Cup to Bourque. Avalanche fans cheered, but so did most National Hockey League (NHL) fans.

For 21 years, Bourque had been a superstar defenseman for the Boston Bruins. He was one of the best in the league for much of that time. But after more than two decades in Boston, Bourque had still not won the Stanley Cup.

In 2000, at age 39, Bourque knew his career was winding down. And he knew the Bruins—the only team he'd ever played for—were struggling. Making the playoffs, much less winning a championship, appeared

A champion at last, Colorado Avalanche defenseman Ray Bourque lifts the Stanley Cup in 2001.

unlikely. So Bourque requested that the Bruins trade him to a team that had a chance to win.

In March 2000 the Bruins did just that, sending their captain to Colorado. With superstar forwards Sakic and Peter Forsberg, plus veteran goalie Patrick Roy, the Avs had the pieces in place to make a run.

With Bourque manning the blue line, the Avs indeed made a run. However, it ended one game short of the Stanley Cup Final. The Dallas Stars beat Colorado in seven games in that year's Western Conference finals.

Bourque was 40 years old that season. But having come so close, he decided to come back and make one more run at the Cup in 2000–01.

This time the Avs couldn't be stopped. They won an NHL-best 52 games during the regular season. In the playoffs, they forced their way past the Vancouver Canucks, Los Angeles Kings, and St. Louis Blues. That set up a Stanley Cup Final against the powerful New Jersey Devils.

In a hard-fought series, Colorado jumped to an early lead only to find itself down three games to two. But a 4–0 shutout in Game 6 sent the series back to Denver for the deciding Game 7. The Avs kept rolling. They scored three goals before New Jersey's first, and that's how the game ended, 3–1.

The long wait was over for Bourque.

That game was the 1,826th of Bourque's NHL career between the regular season and playoffs. It was also his last. Bourque retired a champion, but also as an example of how hard it is to win that trophy.

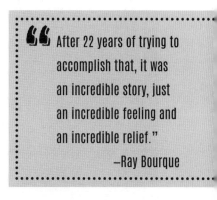

"Joe (Sakic) had an incredible year that year, but I always tell him that's the best assist you ever had, passing me the Cup," Bourque said. "After 22 years of trying to accomplish that, it was an incredible story, just an incredible feeling and an incredible relief."

> After 22 years of trying to accomplish that, it was an incredible story, just an incredible feeling and an incredible relief."
>
> —Ray Bourque

The Stanley Cup has often been referred to as the "most famous trophy in sports." Standing at nearly three feet tall and weighing 34.5 pounds, the Stanley Cup draws a crowd wherever it goes. The Stanley Cup is also one of the oldest trophies in professional team sports, as it has been awarded to hockey champions since 1893. Starting in 1918, the Stanley Cup was given to the champion of the NHL. It still is today.

The Cup has come a long way since Lord Frederick Arthur Stanley, then governor general of Canada,

 The Stanley Cup trophy has changed over the years. The bowl on top is a replica of the original trophy.

came up with the idea that there should be a trophy awarded to that country's hockey champion.

"I have for some time been thinking that it would be a good thing if there were a challenge cup which could be held from year to year by the champion hockey team in the Dominion," Stanley wrote to the Ottawa Athletic Association in 1892.

He later purchased a silver bowl for 10 guineas (equal to about $50 at the time) and created rules for how teams would win this new trophy.

In 1893, it was decided that the champion of the Amateur Hockey Association of Canada would start with the trophy. The first team to claim the Stanley Cup, then known as the Dominion Challenge Trophy, was the Montreal AAA. The AAA won the trophy by finishing the 1893 season with seven wins and just one loss in league play. Two teams challenged the AAA for the title the next year. But the AAA defeated the Montreal Victorias and Ottawa Generals to hold on to the trophy.

Winning back-to-back titles was common in the old days of hockey, but it has become much more difficult in modern times. In fact, the 2017 Pittsburgh Penguins were the first team in nearly 20 years to win back-to-back Stanley Cups. Captain Sidney Crosby led the Penguins to a 4–2 series victory over the Nashville Predators as Pittsburgh earned its second straight Stanley Cup. The last team to win consecutive titles was the Detroit Red Wings in 1997 and 1998.

The Penguins' Stanley Cup win in 2017 was their fifth title overall, but they still have a long way to go to catch the Montreal Canadiens. The NHL's oldest team won the Stanley Cup a record 24 times from 1916 to 1993. Their total through 2017 was 11 more than the next best team, the Toronto Maple Leafs.

A lot of Montreal Canadiens have had their names engraved on the Stanley Cup over the years. That concept began in 1906–07, when the Montreal Wanderers had their names engraved inside the bowl. The tradition didn't catch on right away, but starting in 1924, teams have put the names of each player, coach, owner, and team executive on the Cup. It's one of the traditions that makes the Cup unique. Canadiens legend Henri Richard has had his name on the Cup more times than any other player, having been etched in silver 11 times.

With more than 100 winning teams, it's no surprise that the trophy ran out of room for all of the names. Multiple times. The Hockey Hall of Fame had a solution. Over the years, the Hall started taking bands off the trophy and archiving them to make room for more names.

The battle for the NHL's championship is a grueling two-month marathon called the Stanley Cup Playoffs. There are four rounds, and it takes 16 wins to raise the trophy. Teams can plan on playing as many as 28 games in the playoffs. That's more than one-third as

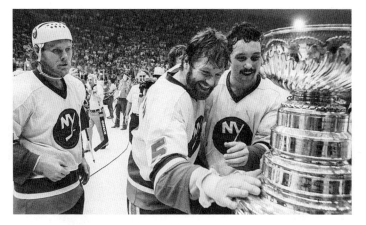

New York Islanders captain Denis Potvin touches the Cup after a long playoff journey in 1980.

many games as are in the entire regular season. The championship series is called the Stanley Cup Final. It has played host to some of the most iconic moments in NHL history. People around the world, but especially in the United States and Canada, tune in every June to see who will claim the Cup.

Many hockey fans will tell you the Cup is one of the toughest trophies to win because of how difficult the playoffs can be, with crushing body checks, blocked shots, and games that can last long into overtime. It takes incredible stamina, toughness, skill, and even a little bit of luck to earn the most prized trophy in the hockey world.

CHAPTER 2

THE BEGINNING

There is some dispute as to where hockey was born, but there's no doubt about where it took on the form we're most familiar with today: Canada. The first recorded indoor hockey game took place on March 3, 1875, in Montreal, Quebec.

From that first indoor game, organized by Canadian James Creighton, hockey spread rapidly throughout the country. Athletic clubs started putting together organized teams and games. Most of the teams were amateur, meaning the players could not get paid. By the 1880s, hockey was a full-blown national phenomenon, which inspired Lord Frederick Arthur Stanley's idea to host a national championship of sorts.

As the game grew in popularity north of the border, it started to take hold in the United States. That was

 The first ice hockey games were played on outdoor rinks around Canada.

especially true in the Upper Peninsula of Michigan, where the world's first fully professional league was born in 1904. It was called the International Hockey League (IHL) and had three teams in Michigan, one in Ontario, and another in Pennsylvania. Canadian stars such as Frederik "Cyclone" Taylor and Edouard "Newsy" Lalonde came to play in the league.

Soon, Canadian amateur leagues got a little tired of losing their best players to this new American league. So they started paying their players, too. The IHL ended up lasting only three seasons, but it set the wheels in motion for professional hockey becoming a bigger deal in Canada. Some of the old amateur clubs began paying their players, and more leagues started sprouting up as citizens of some of the bigger towns and cities sought new forms of entertainment.

From coast to coast in Canada, more leagues began paying players. Amateur teams gave way to professional teams in the battle for the Stanley Cup, with challengers coming from all over Canada.

In 1909–10 a new professional league came along called the National Hockey Association (NHA). It included the Montreal Canadiens, who still exist today as hockey's oldest professional franchise. However, the NHA began losing many of its stars as thousands of young men were being sent overseas to fight for Canada in World War I, which had begun in 1914. It also turned out that the owners in the NHA did not seem to like one another very much.

In particular, the league owners didn't get along with Eddie Livingstone, who owned the Toronto club. So in 1917 the remaining four owners came up with a plan. At meetings held at the Windsor Hotel in Montreal, they decided to form a new league—without Livingstone. That league would be known as the National Hockey League.

The NHL started with just four teams: the Montreal Canadiens, Montreal Wanderers, Ottawa Senators, and Toronto Arenas. It was not the only professional league around, though.

The Pacific Coast Hockey Association (PCHA) had built a great professional league in Western Canada and into the United States. It had teams in British Columbia, one in Seattle, Washington, and another in Portland, Oregon. In fact, the Seattle Metropolitans became the first American team to win the Stanley Cup when they did so in 1917. That league lasted until 1924.

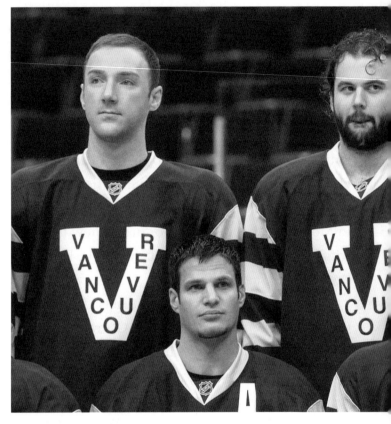

 The Vancouver Canucks wore throwback PCHA Vancouver Millionaires uniforms in 2013.

After the PCHA, there was also the Western Canada Hockey League. It had teams in Alberta, Saskatchewan, and British Columbia. But that league collapsed, too, ending operations in 1926. That left the NHL as the last remaining professional league.

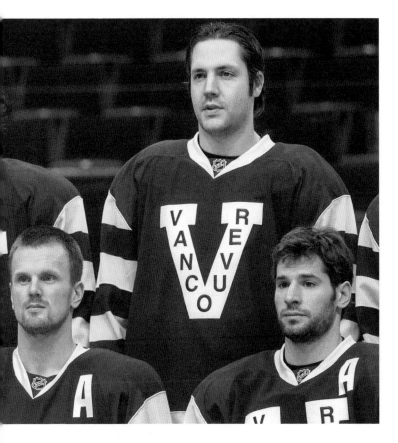

The NHL certainly dealt with some hard times of its own in its early years. Teams were coming and going. Eventually, owners realized that in order to keep the league stable, they would have to expand south of the border and head into the big cities of the United States.

In 1924, the Boston Bruins became the first US team to join the NHL. The following year brought forth the Pittsburgh Pirates hockey club and the New York Americans. In 1926, the Chicago Black Hawks (now Blackhawks), New York Rangers, and Detroit Cougars (now Red Wings) gave the league an even bigger American footprint.

American teams were playing in huge "ice palaces," as they were known at the time. Madison Square Garden in New York and Chicago Stadium, for example, held anywhere from 16,000 to 18,000 fans. This gave professional hockey a better chance to earn enough money to compete with new forms of entertainment such as movies, which were becoming more popular.

Unfortunately for the NHL, the growth stopped abruptly when the Great Depression hit in the late 1920s. Teams struggled to make ends meet. The Ottawa Senators, who had been around since long before the NHL existed, ended up moving to St. Louis before closing down. Also, the Montreal Maroons, Philadelphia Quakers, and Brooklyn Americans all went out of business. By 1942, the NHL had six teams still standing.

 Chicago Black Hawks (from left) Reggie Bentley, Max Bentley, and Doug Bentley pose for a picture in 1942.

The Montreal Canadiens, Toronto Maple Leafs, Boston Bruins, New York Rangers, Detroit Red Wings, and Chicago Black Hawks all survived the Depression. It wasn't easy, but they all found a way. Those six teams then made up the league for the next generation. All six teams still exist today, and they have become known as the Original Six.

CHAPTER 3

THE ORIGINAL SIX

In 2017, the Vegas Golden Knights opened their first season. With that the NHL had 31 teams spread out throughout the United States and Canada. In the early days of the league, no one could have predicted there would be three teams in California and even one in Las Vegas. The fact is, none of that would have been possible without the survival of the six teams that are now affectionately known as the Original Six.

From 1942 to 1967, the Boston Bruins, Chicago Black Hawks, Detroit Red Wings, Montreal Canadiens, New York Rangers, and Toronto Maple Leafs were the only teams in the league. Starting in 1949, when the seasons were extended to 70 games per team, each of the Original Six had to play the others 14 times

Center Ted Kennedy played for the Toronto Maple Leafs from 1942 to 1957.

Montreal's Maurice "Rocket" Richard gets ready to shoot against Chicago Black Hawks goalie Al Rollins in 1954.

apiece in one season. Needless to say, the teams got pretty sick of each other.

Playing the same team so many times made every team a rival. Games became more physical, and fighting was more of a regular part of the game. In one particularly heated matchup in 1955 between Montreal

and Boston—which remains one of hockey's biggest rivalries today—the great Canadiens forward Maurice "Rocket" Richard went after Bruins defenseman Hal Laycoe. In the tussle, Richard ended up punching one of the linesmen trying to break up the fight. Richard was suspended by then NHL president Clarence Campbell for the remainder of the season and playoffs.

A few days later, Campbell attended a game at the Forum in Montreal. Canadiens fans were still terribly mad at him for suspending the team's best player during a season in which they expected to win the Stanley Cup. One fan even came up to Campbell and punched him, setting off a frenzy in the stadium. The chaos spilled into the streets as a riot broke out. It became known as the Maurice Richard Riot. That's how passionate the fans were about these Original Six teams.

Beyond the rivalries, the small number of teams also meant only the very best of the best could make it into the NHL. Of all the people who played hockey in Canada and the United States, only about 150 would see the ice in an NHL game in a given season. So the big stars of that era were really special.

Richard was one of the biggest. He was the first NHL player to score 50 goals in a single season. Back in 1944–45, teams played only 50 games each season, so it was a particularly impressive showing from "Rocket." The Canadiens won eight Stanley Cups during Richard's career, too.

"As soon as (Richard) got the puck at the red line and he focused on the net, you knew no one was going to get the puck off him," said Frank Mahovlich, a Hockey Hall of Famer who starred for the Maple Leafs, Red Wings, and Canadiens.

As big a star as Richard was in Montreal, one of the most important players of the Original Six era was Gordie Howe. He had the perfect mix of skill and toughness to succeed in that era of the game. But as mean as he was on the ice, he was also a gentleman off it. The Red Wings forward became

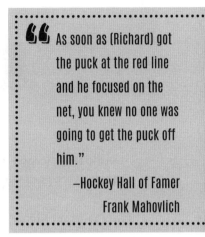

As soon as (Richard) got the puck at the red line and he focused on the net, you knew no one was going to get the puck off him."

—Hockey Hall of Famer Frank Mahovlich

known as "Mr. Hockey" for just that reason. Howe was a fan favorite and one of the biggest attractions in the NHL. He also gave fans plenty to cheer for over his 32 professional seasons, 26 of them in the NHL.

"Gordie Howe is the best," said fellow Hall of Famer Bobby Orr, who played for the Bruins. "Everything you hear about him, there's a little talk about his numbers, but most of it was about what a man he was, what a good person he was, how he treated people. I think that tells who the man is."

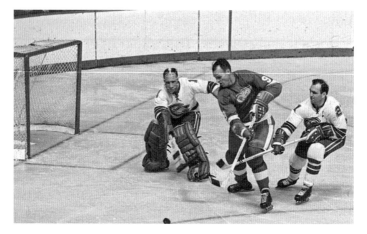

 Gordie Howe (center) was an Original Six star whose career overlapped with the expansion era.

The Original Six era also introduced hockey fans to the NHL's first true dynasties. The Maple Leafs won the Stanley Cup six times between 1942 and 1951. That tremendous success was followed up by an impressive run by Howe's Red Wings, who won three Stanley Cups in four years before giving way to one of the great dynasties in the history of the game. The Canadiens became the first team to win the Stanley Cup five times in a row. Aside from Chicago winning in 1961, Montreal and Toronto kept going back and forth with the Cup for much of the 1960s as well.

Toronto won its last Stanley Cup in 1967, which also marked the end of the Original Six era. For the

1967–68 season, the NHL introduced six new teams as part of its first modern expansion. Joining the Original Six were the Los Angeles Kings, Minnesota North Stars, Oakland Seals, Philadelphia Flyers, Pittsburgh Penguins, and St. Louis Blues.

The expansion era gave rise to new stars such as Orr, a dynamic defenseman for the Bruins. Hard-nosed Flyer Bobby Clarke and slick-scoring forward Marcel Dionne of the Kings also emerged. As the league's popularity grew, so did the NHL itself.

Expansion continued over the coming years. The NHL added teams in cities such as Atlanta, Buffalo, Denver, Kansas City, Vancouver, and Washington, DC, as well as a second team in New York. Even as a rival league called the World Hockey Association (WHA) emerged, the NHL remained strong. And when the WHA eventually folded, the NHL absorbed four of its teams. Just like that, the Edmonton Oilers, Hartford Whalers, Quebec Nordiques, and Winnipeg Jets were NHL teams. After some teams either folded or relocated, the NHL was at 21 teams by 1980.

The arrival of the WHA teams also delivered the NHL its biggest star yet: an 18-year-old from Brantford, Ontario, named Wayne Gretzky.

CHAPTER 4

THE GREAT ONE

When your nickname is simply "The Great One," how could anyone else hope to compare?

Though he retired in 1999, Wayne Gretzky remains one of the most famous hockey players in the world. He holds just about every meaningful offensive record in NHL history. On top of that, Gretzky had as much to do with making hockey more popular in the United States as anyone in the history of the game.

From the time Gretzky was a child, people knew he would be a star. At age 10, he scored 378 goals in a single 85-game season. People were even asking for autographs from Gretzky when he was just a kid.

Gretzky was allowed to play junior hockey at age 14, although most kids don't start at that level until age 16. He played for the Soo Greyhounds in

Wayne Gretzky showcased unique playmaking abilities for the Edmonton Oilers.

Ontario's top junior circuit as a 16-year-old. That's where he wore the number that became iconic across his back. Growing up, Gretzky wore No. 9 as a tribute to his favorite player, Gordie Howe. But a Soo player already had that number, so Gretzky was assigned No. 19 instead. It didn't last. Gretzky soon switched to No. 99, and the rest is history.

"You watch him do things which 10-year NHL veterans have trouble handling, and you figure he must be 35 years old," Hockey Hall of Famer George Armstrong told the *Sporting News* when Gretzky was just 16.

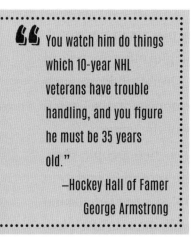

" You watch him do things which 10-year NHL veterans have trouble handling, and you figure he must be 35 years old."

–Hockey Hall of Famer George Armstrong

At age 17, Gretzky was ready for his next step. He signed his first professional contract with the Indianapolis Racers of the WHA. Gretzky ended up playing only eight games with Indianapolis before they traded him to the Edmonton Oilers. The change hardly slowed him down. Gretzky finished his first professional season with 46 goals and 110 points, each ranking third in the league.

30

The following year, the WHA disbanded, and Gretzky's Oilers became part of the NHL. He was an instant success there, too.

Gretzky had 137 points to lead the NHL in his first season in the league. At a time when most people are just finishing high school, he claimed his first Hart Trophy as the league's Most Valuable Player (MVP). The Great One went on to win that trophy a record nine times in his career, more than any other player in history. He also won the Art Ross Trophy as the league's scoring champion 10 times—four more than his idol Howe.

While with Edmonton, Gretzky put up numbers that were once unthinkable to hockey fans. Perhaps the most shocking came in 1981–82. Fans were eager to see if Gretzky could match Maurice Richard's record of 50 goals in 50 games. Instead, Gretzky scored 50 goals in 39 games.

"At the rate he's going he'll break my records in half the time it took me to set them," said Howe, who at the time had the NHL records for most career goals and points, "and I'll be there cheering him on."

Howe couldn't have known how true that prediction would be.

While Gretzky earned numerous accolades and set records that are virtually unbreakable, he also was a part of some amazing teams in Edmonton. The Oilers won four Stanley Cups in a span of just five years, establishing themselves as one of the great dynasties in NHL history. Playing alongside fellow Hall of Famers such as Glenn Anderson, Paul Coffey, Grant Fuhr, Jari Kurri, and Mark Messier, Gretzky led Edmonton to new heights. That's why it was so shocking when he was traded.

One of the lines you'll hear from NHL executives and players sometimes is "If Wayne Gretzky can be traded, anybody can be traded." On August 9, 1988, just months after Gretzky led Edmonton to its fourth Stanley Cup title, the team announced that the game's greatest player had been traded to the Los Angeles Kings. The news stunned the hockey world. Few trades in any sport have been so significant.

The trade was intended to help the Oilers' owner, who was losing money. It also had a huge effect on hockey's growth.

While Edmonton lost its captain and best player, Gretzky went to a major American city. Instantly, the Kings became one of the must-see teams in the NHL, with movie stars and even then-president Ronald

> **Wayne Gretzky brought new life to hockey in Los Angeles, and the United States, after his trade to the Kings.**

Reagan making a point to attend games. Within a few years, Gretzky had the team competing for the Stanley Cup. Though the Kings never ended up winning the title during Gretzky's years there, the impact of the Great One was long lasting.

After going to Los Angeles, Gretzky became one of the biggest celebrities in pro sports. He appeared in commercials, made guest appearances on popular TV shows, hosted *Saturday Night Live*, and was even featured as a character in a popular Saturday morning cartoon alongside Michael Jordan and Bo Jackson.

As Gretzky's popularity exploded, so did the sport's. By the mid-1990s, when Gretzky-mania was reaching its heights in the United States, many cities had built ice rinks just to meet the demand of more people wanting to play hockey. And that wasn't just in California, where Gretzky was the king of the Kings. It was everywhere. NHL commissioner Gary Bettman said that Gretzky's success in California was a big reason why the league expanded yet again. From 1991 to 2000, the league grew from 22 to 30 teams.

Gretzky showed that hockey could work in warm-weather states. The league put two more teams in California and two in Florida, and it saw teams relocate to areas that don't get much snow, such as Arizona, Texas, and North Carolina. Hockey wasn't just a regional game anymore; it had national appeal. A lot of that goes back to the Gretzky trade.

"People paid attention to hockey in places where they might not have focused on it as much, and it was clear there was a great deal of interest in the game," Bettman told the *Canadian Press* on the trade's 25th anniversary. "Wayne's presence in L.A. was the catalyst for that."

In 1999, Gretzky hung up his skates for the final time. By then, he was playing for the New York Rangers. Usually players have to wait three years after retiring before they are eligible for the Hall of

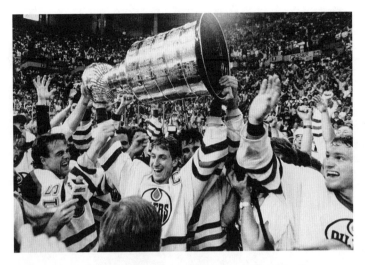

Wayne Gretzky set a standard that all future players are compared with.

Fame. But not Gretzky. The Hall waived his waiting period so he could be inducted immediately. The NHL also retired Gretzky's iconic No. 99 throughout the entire league. He is the only player to have his number retired league-wide.

Before retiring, Gretzky put up 894 goals, 1,963 assists, and 2,857 points. No one has more in any category. In fact, if you included only Gretzky's assists, he'd still have more points than any player in history. Gretzky owns dozens of NHL records and probably will hold most of them forever. There simply will never be another one like the Great One.

CHAPTER 5

THE GREAT DYNASTIES

One team ends each season as the champion. Every once in a while, a team comes around that's so good it wins multiple championships in a short period of time. These teams are called dynasties.

In the NHL's history, different dynasties have defined the league for certain eras. In the Original Six days, the Toronto Maple Leafs became the league's first dynasty. Beginning in 1942, the Leafs won six Stanley Cups in 10 seasons.

Toronto soon gave way to its rival, the Montreal Canadiens. With separate periods of dominance in the 1950s, 1960s, and 1970s, the Habs have had multiple

Toronto Maple Leafs captain Syl Apps celebrates the 1942 Stanley Cup, the team's first of six in 10 seasons.

dynasties. Altogether the team has won 24 Stanley Cups, which is far and away the most.

Building a dynasty today, however, has become harder than ever. In the past, teams could spend freely on players. Now they're limited by a salary cap, which makes it harder to sign a lot of great players. Players have more opportunities to switch teams via free agency, too. Meanwhile, the league keeps growing, and teams are constantly reloading so they can make a run at the Cup. Despite this, teams like the Chicago Blackhawks and Pittsburgh Penguins have established dynasties of their own.

Here are some of the great dynasties in league history.

TORONTO MAPLE LEAFS (1942–51)

Young fans might not think of the Maple Leafs as big winners. After all, the team's last Stanley Cup win came in 1967. For a time, though, Toronto was the envy of all the Original Six teams.

In 1942, the Leafs beat the Detroit Red Wings in seven games to win the Cup. It was a preview of things to come. Beginning with the 1944–45 season, Toronto won the Stanley Cup five of the next seven seasons. At that point, no team in the NHL era had won three straight titles. Toronto did it in 1947, 1948, and 1949. In doing so, the Leafs established themselves as the NHL's first real dynasty.

Talented center Ted "Teeder" Kennedy and fierce goalie Turk Broda were on all five Leafs Stanley Cup teams. The Leafs also got significant contributions from center Syl Apps for two of those Stanley Cups. He probably would have been around for the others, but he was serving in the Canadian military during World War II (1939–1945) for two years. He retired after Toronto won the Cup in 1948.

MONTREAL CANADIENS (1956–60, 1965–71, 1976–79)

Throughout their history, the Canadiens have rarely had just one good season. In 1931, the team won its second Stanley Cup of the NHL era—and it came one year after winning its first. From 1944 to 1946, the Habs won two in three years. Then things really got going.

After winning again in 1953, the Canadiens began the most dominant stretch in NHL history three years later. Led by Maurice "Rocket" Richard, the graceful-skating Jean Beliveau, the hard-shooting Bernie "Boom Boom" Geoffrion, the brilliant defenseman Doug Harvey, and revolutionary goalie Jacques Plante, Montreal won the Cup again in 1956. Then it added another one in 1957. And then came not one, not two, but three more. When the run ended in 1960, the Canadiens had signed their names to the Cup five years in a row. No team before or after has matched that.

Richard retired after the last of the five straight Cups. But Beliveau stayed around, becoming the new leader of the team. And soon enough, another dynasty emerged. From 1965 to 1971, Montreal won five more Stanley Cups. Those teams also included such greats as Yvan Cournoyer, Jacques Lemaire, Guy Lapointe, Henri "Pocket Rocket" Richard, and later young goalie Ken Dryden. Like Maurice Richard, Beliveau retired a champion with his name on the Stanley Cup 10 times as a player.

The last great Canadiens dynasty came in the late 1970s. Scotty Bowman had coached the St. Louis Blues to three Stanley Cup Finals in the late 1960s, but his expansion Blues came up short each time. Bowman's luck changed in Montreal. After he led Montreal to the Cup in 1973, the Habs won four straight from 1976 to 1979.

Those teams had some incredible Hall of Fame players, such as Dryden, the skilled Guy Lafleur, and

**Jean Beliveau (center) was part of 10
Stanley Cup–winning teams from 1951 to 1971.**

Larry Robinson, one of the all-time great defensemen.
Dryden retired after the last Cup in 1979 at just 31
years old. In eight years with the team, he won the
Stanley Cup six times.

In full, the Canadiens' entire first 80 years was
almost like one long dynasty. They won their first
Stanley Cup title in 1916. They added 13 more between
1956 and 1979. And after goalie Patrick Roy led the

team to its last win in 1993, Montreal had an amazing 24 Stanley Cups. No other team came close.

NEW YORK ISLANDERS (1980–83)

The first part of the 1980s was all about the Islanders. Led by legendary coach Al Arbour and goal-scoring stud Mike Bossy, the Isles won four Cups in a row, from 1980 to 1983. While Bossy was the face of the team, he had plenty of help. Offensive defenseman Denis Potvin, gifted playmaker Bryan Trottier, and fearsome goalie Billy Smith were also key players as the Islanders steamrolled through the league.

Losing to the Islanders in the 1983 Cup Final helped the Edmonton Oilers understand what true greatness was. "We walked by (the Islanders') locker room in the corridor and saw after they won they were too beat up to really enjoy it and savor the victory at that moment," Wayne Gretzky recalled. "We were able to walk out of there pretty much scot-free. We had so much respect for the Islanders players and the Islanders teams that we learned immediately you have to take it to another level in order to win a Stanley Cup."

Of all the teams that came after Montreal's 1950s dynasty, the Islanders came closest to matching the Canadiens' five consecutive wins. However,

 New York Islanders right wing Mike Bossy scored at least 50 goals in each of his first nine seasons.

New York's bid for No. 5 ended in the Stanley Cup Final. An upstart Oilers dynasty was just beginning.

EDMONTON OILERS (1984–90)

Led by the great Wayne Gretzky, the Oilers of the early 1980s appeared on their way to dominance. But there were some hiccups along the way.

In 1982, the upstart Oilers were upset by the Los Angeles Kings in the first round of the playoffs. The next year, Edmonton got all the way to the Cup Final but lost to the Islanders. After that, though, the Oilers were ready to roll.

With Gretzky and center Mark Messier leading the way, Edmonton overpowered its opponents offensively. In 1984, the Oilers got revenge on the Islanders to win their first Stanley Cup. They then went on to win three of the next four, cementing their status as one of the NHL's most iconic dynasties.

Aside from Gretzky and Messier, those Oilers teams featured Hall of Famers such as Paul Coffey, Jari Kurri, Glenn Anderson, and Grant Fuhr. The Oilers also added one more Stanley Cup to their trophy cabinet in 1990, two years after Gretzky had been traded to the Kings.

What made these Oilers teams so special was how much offense they could produce. Gretzky and Kurri were an unstoppable duo. Coffey was one of the best offensive defensemen of his or any era. Messier and Anderson were routinely hitting 100 points. Teams just could not slow them down.

MORE DYNASTIES

Since the 1990s, dynasties have been scarcer. But a couple of teams have had memorable runs.

Sidney Crosby and the Penguins show off the Stanley Cup during their 2017 victory parade in Pittsburgh.

The Detroit Red Wings won back-to-back Stanley Cups in 1997 and 1998. Beginning in 2010, the Chicago Blackhawks won three Stanley Cups in six years. Meanwhile, the Pittsburgh Penguins won a pair of Stanley Cups in 2016 and 2017. These teams might be the closest we will ever come to seeing a dynasty like those of yesteryear.

45

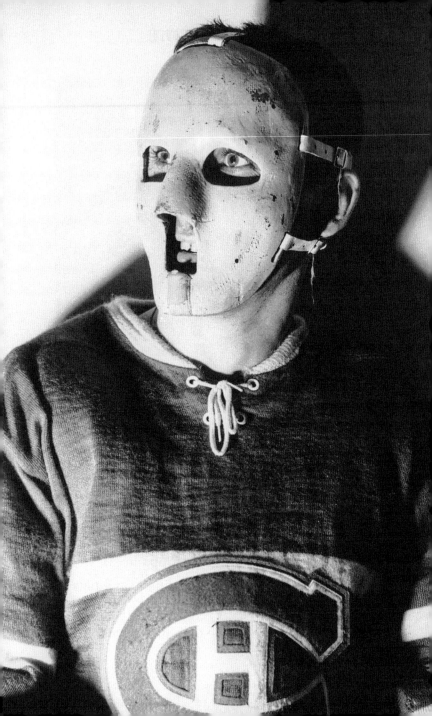

CHAPTER 6

MASKED MEN:
THE GREATEST GOALIES
OF ALL TIME

Hockey players can shoot a puck upwards of 105 miles per hour, sometimes faster if it catches the right deflection. While players haven't always shot it that hard, a hard shot still sends a hockey puck flying through the air at a high rate of speed. And until November 1, 1959, not a single goalie had ever worn a mask in a game. Montreal Canadiens star Jacques Plante changed that.

Plante had been using a mask in practice, but never in a game. However, on that fateful night in 1959, the Canadiens were playing the New York Rangers. In the

Although Jacques Plante introduced goalie masks, his version offered little protection compared with those used today.

first period, the Rangers' Andy Bathgate sent a tricky backhanded shot toward Montreal's goal. Plante got in front of it. Unfortunately, he got in front of it with his face.

The goalie was badly bloodied. The game was delayed for more than 20 minutes. Then, finally, Plante was ready. He'd come back into the game, he told coach Toe Blake, if he could wear his mask.

This might seem an obvious decision now. Back then, though, the thought of a mask was unheard of. Blake had previously rejected the idea altogether. But teams didn't even have backup goalies at the time. So when pressed with the choice of Plante playing or sitting, Blake gave in. The Hall of Fame goalie returned to the ice, this time wearing his mask.

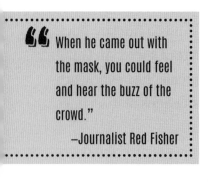

When he came out with the mask, you could feel and hear the buzz of the crowd."
—Journalist Red Fisher

"When he came out with the mask, you could feel and hear the buzz of the crowd," journalist Red Fisher recalled.

Montreal won the game, and Plante never looked back. It took a few more years for masks to fully catch on with other goalies, but the mask became the goalie's most iconic piece of equipment. Netminders are even referred to as "The Masked Men."

Today Plante is most famous for his mask, but he was also one heck of a goalie. In Montreal history, he was one of many.

Georges Vezina, the Canadiens' first great goalie, played for the team even before it entered the NHL. Fans might recognize the name. Today the trophy given to the NHL's best goalie every year is named for Vezina.

Several Canadiens goalies have won that award over the years. Nobody has won more than Plante's seven. But Montreal's Bill Durnan won the first of six in 1944, Ken Dryden won the first of his five in 1973, and then Patrick Roy won three, beginning in 1989.

Roy was one of the most successful goalies in NHL history, and he played during a time when goal scoring was at its highest. The Quebec native burst into the league during the 1985–86 season. As a 20-year-old rookie, he backstopped the Canadiens to the Stanley Cup and won the Conn Smythe Trophy as playoffs MVP. Known for his fierce competitiveness and fiery personality, Roy ended up winning four Stanley Cups—two with Montreal and two with the Colorado

 Montreal's Patrick Roy gets in position to make a save against the Ottawa Senators in 1995.

Avalanche. He is the only player to have won the Conn Smythe Trophy three times, although that award has only been handed out since 1965. Additionally, Roy is second all-time in wins by a goaltender with 551.

"I think he perfected the position, personally," said former NHL goaltender Darren Pang.

Not all great goalies played in Montreal. Terry Sawchuk played 21 seasons in the NHL, including 14 with the Detroit Red Wings. In the Original Six era, there might not have been a better goalie. At the end of his career, Sawchuk was the NHL's leader in games played, wins, and shutouts. Former Red Wings teammate Alex Delvecchio joked that "you couldn't put a pea past" Sawchuk. He won the Vezina Trophy four times and helped the Red Wings win three Stanley Cups in four years.

In the 1990s, Dominik Hasek earned his reputation as "The Dominator." Born in Czechoslovakia, he set a new standard for European goalies in the NHL. Hasek won the Vezina six times while playing for the Buffalo Sabres. He was also a five-time finalist for the Hart Trophy, given to the league's MVP, and the only goaltender to win it twice.

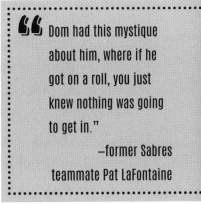

" Dom had this mystique about him, where if he got on a roll, you just knew nothing was going to get in."

–former Sabres teammate Pat LaFontaine

"Dom had this mystique about him, where if he got on a roll, you just knew nothing was going to get in," said former Sabres teammate Pat LaFontaine.

Hasek had some of the best reflexes in the game and could make incredible saves while flopping all over the ice. He would do anything to stop a puck, sometimes dropping his goalie stick if he thought it gave him a better chance to make a save. It worked a lot. After coming close to a Cup with the Sabres once in 1999, Hasek ended up winning two Stanley Cups with the Detroit Red Wings before retiring in 2008 at age 43.

For all of their skill, Roy and Hasek had competition for the title of the best goalie of their generation. Martin Brodeur played parts of 21 seasons with the New Jersey Devils, rewriting many of the NHL's goalie records in the process.

While in New Jersey, Brodeur won three Stanley Cups, four Vezina Trophies, and the Calder Trophy as the 1993–94 rookie of the year. Brodeur set the NHL goalie records for games played (1,266), wins (691), and shutouts (125), among others. Brodeur also was an excellent puck handler, a skill not every goalie possesses. He actually scored three empty-net goals in his career, including one in a playoff game. Brodeur also was credited with 45 assists, which is among the most all-time by a goalie.

The NHL is always changing. But good goalies still have the potential to be game changers. In recent years, goalies such as Carey Price and Henrik

The New York Rangers' Henrik Lundqvist blocks a puck from the butterfly position in 2018.

Lundqvist have led the way. Price became the 13th Montreal goalie to win the Vezina Trophy when he did so in 2014–15. Meanwhile, down in New York, Lundqvist has become known as "The King" or "King Henrik." Lundqvist has put up some of the best numbers of any goalie in the modern NHL. He also helped his native Sweden win the 2006 Olympic gold medal, and he won the Vezina in 2011–12.

CHAPTER 7

LEGENDS AND HEROES

Wayne Gretzky might have been the game's brightest star, but the NHL's history has been dotted with players who have captured the imaginations of hockey fans.

It all started with Howie Morenz, largely considered the game's first true star. Morenz played 12 seasons for the Montreal Canadiens, beginning in 1923, before brief stints with the Chicago Black Hawks and New York Rangers. Known for his tremendous skating speed and offensive abilities, Morenz won three Stanley Cups with Montreal. He also earned the Hart Trophy as the NHL MVP three times. With 472 points in 550 games, he was the kind of player who even opposing fans wanted to see.

 Center Howie Morenz starred for the Montreal Canadiens from 1923 to 1934, and then finished his career there in 1936–37.

55

The American press took to calling Morenz the "Babe Ruth of Hockey," and some credit him with saving professional hockey when its popularity started to weaken, even in Canada. Sadly, Morenz died five weeks after suffering a broken leg in what was his final NHL game in 1937. Blood clots that developed due to the severe injury were believed to be the cause of his death. His funeral was held in the Canadiens' stadium. Approximately 10,000 mourners attended. Thousands more lined the streets for his procession to the cemetery where he was laid to rest. Eight years later, he was part of the first class inducted into the Hockey Hall of Fame.

Morenz was part of a long line of stars that played for the Canadiens. Maurice "Rocket" Richard was one of the players who reminded Montreal fans most of Morenz. Richard broke into the NHL in 1942. In 1944–45, he became the first NHL player to reach 50 goals. No other player, including Richard, hit that mark until Bernie Geoffrion scored 50 in 1960–61. Who did he play for? You guessed it: the Canadiens. Richard's goal scoring was so revered that the leading goal scorer in the NHL receives the Rocket Richard Trophy at the end of each season.

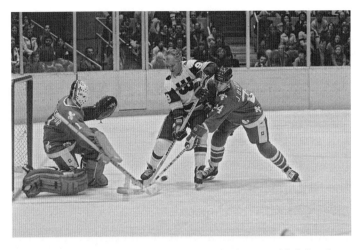

> Gordie Howe (center) was still playing at a high level years after his peers had retired.

Four years after Richard entered the NHL, Gordie Howe broke in with the Detroit Red Wings. By the time he was 18 years old, his talent was obvious. But no one could have predicted he'd play into his 50s.

Known affectionately the world over as "Mr. Hockey," Howe was both a great scorer and tough as nails. He won both the league scoring title and the Hart Trophy six times each. Only Gretzky was named MVP more times. The Red Wings won four Stanley Cups with Howe on their roster.

Yet Howe's most impressive characteristic might have been his longevity. He is the only NHL player who played in five different decades. His first game was in 1946, and his last was in 1980. That's a record that will likely never be matched.

During that time, Howe played in an NHL record 1,767 games. Only Gretzky scored more than Howe's 801 goals. Those NHL numbers become even more impressive when you consider that Howe retired from the NHL in 1971. After staying retired for two seasons, he signed with the Houston Aeros and spent six years playing in the WHA, a short-lived competitor to the NHL. When the WHA shut down, Howe played one more year in the NHL. Amazingly, even at 51 years old, he had 41 points in 80 games for the Hartford Whalers in that final season.

Though many would say Gretzky is the greatest of all time, "The Great One" often points to Howe as the greatest player ever to play the game.

"Two things separated Gordie from everyday players," Gretzky said. "One, Gordie never thought he was bigger or better than anybody else. He always wanted to prove that he was. He never said to anybody, 'I'm the best player, I'm the No. 1 guy.' And he always had a need to perform each and every game and practice. That's what separated Gordie Howe from the rest, and that's why he was Gordie Howe. He had a definite ambition that he was going to be the best player every night and every year. That's how he lived. He never changed."

Some great players dominate the game. Others change the game. The latter can be said about legendary Boston Bruins defenseman Bobby Orr.

When Orr debuted as an 18-year-old in 1966–67, defensemen had a clear role. They were supposed to defend. They could pitch in on offense, but would they ever lead their team in scoring? That'd be a shock. Then Orr came along.

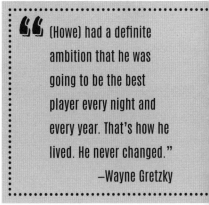

> ❝ (Howe) had a definite ambition that he was going to be the best player every night and every year. That's how he lived. He never changed."
> —Wayne Gretzky

At age 21, Orr led the NHL in scoring with 120 points in 1969–70. The next year he had 102 assists and 139 points. He won another scoring title in 1974–75 with 135 points. Orr finished his career with a stunning 915 points in 657 games.

Perhaps Orr's name would fill the record books more had injuries not cut short his career. But what an

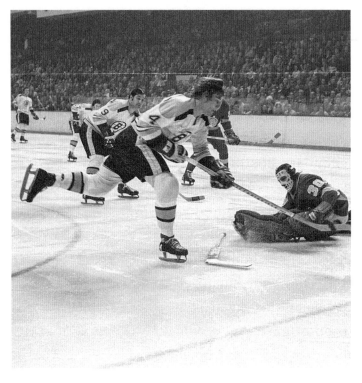

 The Boston Bruins' Bobby Orr blasts a shot on the Los Angeles Kings' goal in 1972.

impact he had while he was there. He won the Norris Trophy as the league's top defenseman a record eight times. He also became the only defenseman to win the Hart Trophy more than once, having been named MVP three times.

"The challenge, of course, was trying to find ways to stop (Orr)," recalled former Philadelphia Flyers captain Bobby Clarke. "We used to try different things. None of them worked."

As much as Orr is remembered for his brilliant career, he is perhaps most famous for the goal he scored in the 1970 Stanley Cup Final. With the Bruins and St. Louis Blues stuck in overtime, Orr snuck into the zone and got a perfect pass from Derek Sanderson. In an instant, he slipped the puck under Blues goalie Glenn Hall. As the puck crossed the line, Orr was tripped and sent flying through the air. The image of Orr celebrating while flying through the air captured by photographer Ray Lussier is one of the most famous photographs in hockey history. But most important, Orr's goal gave Boston its first Stanley Cup since 1941.

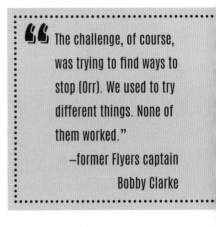

> The challenge, of course, was trying to find ways to stop (Orr). We used to try different things. None of them worked."
> —former Flyers captain Bobby Clarke

Just as Orr was wrapping up his career, Gretzky came in to fill the void. However, it would be a few more years before Gretzky had a worthy opponent for the title of best player in the world. That came in the form of Pittsburgh Penguins center Mario Lemieux. On top of being supremely talented, Lemieux was also a giant. At 6-foot-4 and 230 pounds, he was like a linebacker on skates with quick hands and creativity.

Gretzky was the better playmaker, but Lemieux was a more natural goal scorer. He won scoring titles in six different seasons. Lemieux might have won more, too, if he hadn't suffered from horrible back problems. He even had a bout with cancer, but he beat it and was able to continue his career.

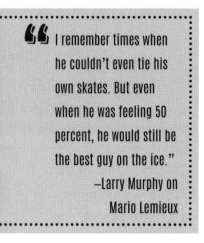

I remember times when he couldn't even tie his own skates. But even when he was feeling 50 percent, he would still be the best guy on the ice."
–Larry Murphy on Mario Lemieux

"I remember times when he couldn't even tie his own skates," said former teammate Larry Murphy. "But even when he was feeling 50 percent, he would still be the best guy on the ice."

These men helped pave the way for today's stars such as Sidney Crosby, Alex Ovechkin, Erik Karlsson, and Connor McDavid, who continue to thrill hockey fans around the world.

 The Edmonton Oilers are hoping Connor McDavid can follow Wayne Gretzky's path to superstardom.

CHAPTER 8

THE WINTER CLASSIC

It was New Years Day 2008. The snow fell onto the ice surface set up in the middle of Ralph Wilson Stadium, home of the National Football League's Buffalo Bills. Pittsburgh Penguins star Sidney Crosby, the fresh face of the NHL, skated to center ice. If he managed to score on Buffalo Sabres goalie Ryan Miller, his Penguins would win the first ever NHL Winter Classic.

It had been snowing steadily almost the entire game, leaving the ice coated with fresh powder. Those aren't the best circumstances for a player to handle the puck, and they definitely don't make it any easier for the goaltender trying to watch his opponent's

 Buffalo Sabres goalie Ryan Miller wears a cap to stay warm during the 2008 Winter Classic.

 The 2008 Winter Classic brought professional hockey into the elements.

every move. Crosby was confident, though. As the Penguins' captain neared the net, he started making his moves. When Miller moved to his right, Crosby saw an opening and slid the puck between the goaltender's legs. As the puck hit the back of the net, Crosby let out a "Wooooo!" loud enough to be picked up by the

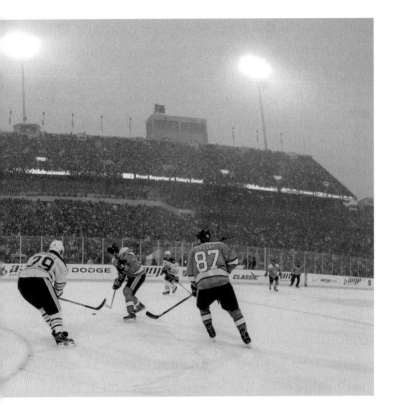

TV microphones. The stadium fell silent for a moment as the Penguins celebrated their thrilling win in a now iconic moment.

Hockey was born outdoors, on frozen ponds and lakes. As bodies of water froze across Canada and the northern United States each winter, people put on their skates and began playing hockey. Outdoor games helped the game grow during the late 1800s and early 1900s. So in 2008 the league decided to go back to its roots and play in the open air.

The NHL was actually beaten to the punch on the outdoor game concept. Back in 2001, Michigan State's men's hockey team hosted archrival Michigan at the school's football stadium. More than 74,000 people came to the game, making it the largest crowd ever to attend a hockey game at that time. Two years later, the NHL held its first regular-season outdoor game in Edmonton between the Oilers and the Montreal Canadiens. The game, called the Heritage Classic, was a big success, too, but it seemed as if it would be only a one-time event.

The idea to make the Winter Classic an annual event came from NBC executive Jon Miller. He was inspired while watching a baseball game, of all things. Miller thought to himself that it would be interesting for NHL teams to play in the most famous stadiums in sports, such as baseball's Yankee Stadium. He brought the idea to the NHL. It took a few years, but soon plans started for the first Winter Classic in Buffalo.

From that first game in snowy Buffalo to today, the Winter Classic has been a huge hit. It is the NHL's most-watched regular-season game each year, in terms of both fans in the seats and viewers watching on television. For that very first Winter Classic, 3.75 million people tuned in to see Crosby's shootout heroics.

"When you see 70,000 people jammed into a stadium to watch hockey, it's a good sign," Crosby told the reporters after the game. "The atmosphere and environment, I don't think you can beat that."

The next two Winter Classics were held in the iconic baseball stadiums Miller had dreamed about. The 2009 Winter Classic was held at Chicago's Wrigley Field. Boston's Fenway Park hosted the 2010 event.

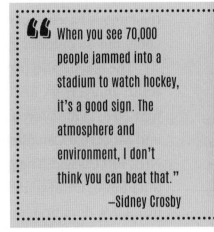

When you see 70,000 people jammed into a stadium to watch hockey, it's a good sign. The atmosphere and environment, I don't think you can beat that."
—Sidney Crosby

The biggest Winter Classic came in 2014. More than 100,000 hockey fans braved frigid temperatures and heavy snow to pack Michigan Stadium, home of the Michigan Wolverines football team. With snow falling onto the ice, the Toronto Maple Leafs defeated the Detroit Red Wings 3–2 in a shootout.

With the success of the Winter Classic, the NHL began hosting more outdoor games. These games are part of the league's Stadium Series. The first of those games, in 2014, was different from any Winter Classic. That's because it was the first to be played in a warm climate. The Anaheim Ducks beat the host Los Angeles Kings 3–0 while playing at Dodger Stadium. Despite highs in the mid-70s Fahrenheit (low 20s Celsius), the cooling equipment kept the ice in good condition at the famous baseball park. That game proved the NHL could put an outdoor game just about anywhere.

The league also played outdoors to celebrate its 100th anniversary in 2017–18. To commemorate the first NHL game played in 1917, the Ottawa Senators and Montreal Canadiens played a game called the NHL 100 Classic. The game was played at TD Place Stadium in Ottawa on December 16, 2017. That was just a few days prior to the exact 100th anniversary of the NHL's first game, which also featured Montreal and a different team from Ottawa.

The Winter Classic, Heritage Classic, and Stadium Series games have generated newfound fan interest for the league. Fans are eager to learn which huge or iconic stadium might host the game next. The

 Fans filled baseball's iconic Fenway Park for the 2010 Winter Classic between the Boston Bruins and the Philadelphia Flyers.

league has also considered hosting games in other nontraditional settings, such as at Parliament Hill in Canada or the National Mall in Washington, DC. Wherever it goes next, people will surely be watching what has become one of the NHL's signature events.

CHAPTER 9

THE PATH TO THE NHL

The 2015 NHL Entry Draft was one of the most anticipated in a decade. Some years there is one player everybody wants, a player who is sure to change the fortunes of his team. In 2015, there were two of them. Everybody wanted to see whether the Edmonton Oilers would pick Connor McDavid or Jack Eichel with the first overall pick.

Both men were high-scoring players from opposite sides of the border, with McDavid a Canadian and Eichel an American. They also represented two of the most prominent paths players take to the NHL: junior hockey and college hockey.

Jack Eichel went to Boston University rather than a junior league to continue his development.

Hockey has a unique development pipeline as compared with other popular sports. Pro basketball and football players usually suit up for their high school and college teams first. But that's not a given in hockey. In fact, many North American players never play for a college or even a high school team. Instead, they develop their skills with junior teams.

Junior teams are for players aged 16 to 20. There are different leagues that play at different levels throughout Canada and the United States. Oftentimes, players move to a new city to play for a junior league. They live with a host family and attend classes at a local school while also playing with top players from their age group. It can be a challenging transition, but the level of play can be so high that it's usually worth it.

This is the path McDavid took. Growing up in Ontario, McDavid stood out as a player from a young age. The Ontario Hockey League (OHL) is one of the most competitive junior leagues. In 2012, it accepted McDavid when he was only 15 years old. The teenager joined the Erie Otters in Pennsylvania. His performances against bigger and older players only confirmed what scouts had already known: he was really good.

"He's as good as I've seen in the last 30 years," Wayne Gretzky told the *Edmonton Journal* in McDavid's draft year.

Eichel, meanwhile, followed a different path. Growing up in Massachusetts, he was noticed by USA Hockey scouts. They invited him to play at the US National Team Development Program in Michigan. Teams in that program play against older junior and college opponents. That helped Eichel gain more confidence. From there, he went back home and played one season for Boston University. Named the Hobey Baker Award winner as the best player in college hockey, Eichel was ready for the next step.

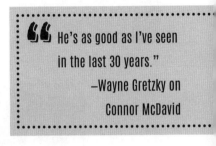

" He's as good as I've seen in the last 30 years."
—Wayne Gretzky on Connor McDavid

At the NHL Draft, the Oilers selected McDavid. Eichel went second overall to the Buffalo Sabres. To most observers, the two teams were both winners in that draft.

McDavid and Eichel represent two unique paths to the NHL. But in today's global game, there are endless possibilities for reaching the league. In 2004, junior Blake Wheeler helped his Breck School team

 Filip Forsberg (left) scored 31 goals for the Nashville Predators in 2016–17 before helping lead them to the Stanley Cup Final.

win the Minnesota high school state title. Then he played one year of junior hockey and three years at the University of Minnesota. The next season, he made his NHL debut. In 2016, the Winnipeg Jets named him team captain.

There are also NHL players from all over Europe. Many of them grow up playing for hometown clubs. For example, Nashville Predators star Filip Forsberg played for the Leksands IF club in Sweden. He stayed with the club from the youth hockey level all the way to his debut with its professional team when he was just 16. Although the Washington Capitals drafted him in 2012, Forsberg stayed to play one more season in Sweden. He was eventually traded to the Nashville Predators and made his NHL debut at the end of the 2012–13 season.

Regardless of how they develop, most NHL players join the league through the NHL Entry Draft. The draft is held every year in late June. Players who will be at least 18 years old by the start of training camp of the next NHL season are eligible to be picked in the draft. The draft lasts seven rounds with 31 picks in each round. At the end, approximately 217 players will be selected. But not every player drafted ends up making it to the NHL. In fact, many don't.

NHL teams have large staffs of scouts who travel the globe trying to find players with NHL talent. It's a difficult job to try to predict which players will be NHL players, and it's even harder to predict which of them will become stars in the league. Sometimes scouts have to go to remote towns in Russia or prep school games in Massachusetts or low-level junior leagues in Canada. They try to leave no stone unturned in finding the next stars.

While players like McDavid, Eichel, Wheeler, and Forsberg were all first-round picks who went on to NHL success, not all top prospects pan out as expected. The Ottawa Senators hoped Alexandre Daigle would turn into a star when they picked him first overall in 1993. Instead, he bounced around teams and leagues, never becoming much more than a role player.

Meanwhile, some of the NHL's best players were drafted very low. Former Detroit Red Wings defenseman Nicklas Lidstrom was the 53rd player picked in his draft year of 1989. Yet no player in his draft year played more games or had more assists than Lidstrom. He is now considered one of the greatest defensemen in the history of the game.

One of Lidstrom's former Red Wings teammates was picked much lower. Pavel Datsyuk was the 171st overall choice in the 1998 NHL Draft. Datsyuk, who earned the nickname "The Magic Man" for his great puck handling, had 918 points in his career and helped Detroit win two Stanley Cups.

And some players aren't drafted at all. Martin St. Louis was a star in college at Vermont. But at

 After being drafted in the sixth round, Pavel Datsyuk played 14 seasons for the Detroit Red Wings.

5-foot-8, he was a smaller player. No NHL teams picked him in the draft. Instead, he signed as a free agent with the Calgary Flames in 1998. He went on to play more than 1,000 games in the NHL while scoring more than 1,000 points. His career also included a Hart Memorial Trophy and the 2004 Stanley Cup with the Tampa Bay Lightning.

It just goes to show that there is no one way to make it into the NHL.

CHAPTER 10

CREATING THE PERFECT HOCKEY PLAYER

To make it to the NHL, you have to be able to do a lot of things better than almost anyone else in the world and do them all on ice. To become a star, you have to be the best of the best in at least one particular skill and still be excellent in everything else.

So let's think about all of the skills necessary to become an NHL star, particularly for forwards and defensemen. There's never been a player, not even Wayne Gretzky, who was the very best at every single skill. What if we could take the best skills from some of

Connor McDavid's skating ability helps him find separation from defenders on the ice.

81

the game's biggest stars of the past and today's game and put them into one player? What if we could build the perfect hockey player? What would that look like?

What our player physically looks like probably doesn't matter. Size might matter a little, but there are more important skills to consider. This is all about what kind of skills we can give a person to help him become the best that ever was.

So let's start building from the ground up.

SKATING: CONNOR MCDAVID

Especially in today's NHL, speed is incredibly important. Teams are always trying to get faster. There is probably nobody faster than McDavid. The Edmonton Oilers' captain has shown that he can blow by defenders with ease thanks to the explosiveness that comes from his legs.

Since McDavid is so fast, he gets a lot of breakaways in games where it is just him against the goalie. Nobody can catch up. In fact, McDavid was once clocked skating at 25 miles per hour on an end-to-end rush that resulted in a goal. That's comparable to track legend Usain Bolt's fastest recorded running speed.

 Alex Ovechkin's powerful shot ensures the Washington Capitals are always a dangerous scoring team.

SHOT: ALEX OVECHKIN

There have been many great shooters over the years, but one of the greatest goal scorers of all time is still playing today. Ovechkin's shot might not be the hardest among all players, but it is probably the most accurate. Whether with a slap shot or a wrist shot, Ovechkin can be deadly when he has enough space to shoot. The Russian superstar was the NHL's top goal scorer for the seventh time in 2017–18. He also led the league in shots on goal for the 11th time.

"Some guys in the league just shoot quick and some guys shoot hard and heavy," NHL goalie Pascal Leclaire told the *Washington Post*. "His shot has both."

STICK HANDLING: PAVEL DATSYUK

There are a lot of great players that have been experts at handling the puck, but only one was ever called "The Magic Man." That would be Datsyuk, who played 14 seasons with the Detroit Red Wings before retiring in 2016. He earned that nickname for his tremendous ability with the puck on his stick.

Datsyuk made many defensemen look foolish on some of his best moves. His incredibly quick hands made him difficult to defend. They also made him an expert in stealing the puck from his opponents. He was a complete player and exciting to watch all at the same time.

DEFENSIVE SKILLS: LARRY ROBINSON

As important as it is to score goals, you have to prevent them as well. Playing good defense in hockey usually takes a strong player who is always in position and always looking to get the puck from the other team. It takes a combination of smarts, strength, and quick decision making.

Robinson was a star for the Montreal Canadiens in the 1970s. He impressed his teammates with his toughness and his ability to control a game. He could score with the best of them, but he was always about protecting his net first. Robinson finished his career with an NHL record plus-730 rating, meaning in even-strength situations he was on the ice for 730 more goals for his team than for the opposition. No player is even close to that record.

TOUGHNESS: GORDIE HOWE

Hockey is a contact sport, after all. That means you have to have quite a bit of toughness and courage to play the game at the highest levels. One of the best examples of such a mix was Howe. "Mr. Hockey" was one of the game's greatest scorers, but he was best known for being a ferocious competitor who played the game hard and never backed down from anyone. It also takes toughness to play as long as Howe did. His career started in 1946 and ended in 1980.

Playing tough can get you into trouble sometimes, though. Howe had 1,685 penalty minutes in his NHL career. Also, it is still called a "Gordie Howe Hat Trick" when a player records at least one goal, one assist, and one fight in a game.

LEADERSHIP: MARK MESSIER

To win hockey games you need a strong team, and behind a strong team is usually a strong leader. There have been few better leaders than Messier, who became the first player to captain two different teams to the Stanley Cup. He once famously guaranteed his New York Rangers would win Game 6 of the Eastern Conference finals in 1994. Then Messier scored a hat trick against the New Jersey Devils to make good on his promise. The Rangers went on to win their first Stanley Cup since 1940 just a few weeks later.

The NHL thinks so highly of Messier's leadership that the league has established an end-of-season award for captains. The Mark Messier Leadership Award goes to individuals who are viewed as superior leaders in their sport.

"He has to go down as one of the best all-time leaders in any professional sport," former Oilers coach John Muckler said.

HOCKEY SENSE: WAYNE GRETZKY

Hockey sense is a term scouts and coaches use to describe a number of things, like how a player sees the ice, the decisions the player makes with the puck, and how they process the game. It all comes back to the

 Oilers teammates Mark Messier (left) and Wayne Gretzky (right) lift the Stanley Cup in 1988.

brain. Ask anyone why Gretzky was so good, and they won't say it was about his size or his physical skills. It was about his mind.

Gretzky could see how plays were going to develop before they actually did, and he had a great feel for the game. He was just smarter than the opposition at all times.

"Wayne played chess, and he was playing, five, six, seven, ten, twenty moves ahead of everybody else," former teammate Messier once said.

CHAPTER 11

INNOVATION AND THE EVOLUTION OF THE NHL

Hockey has evolved a lot over the years to become the game you see today. Just think: in the very beginning, if you didn't live near a large body of water in a colder climate where the water froze, you couldn't play hockey. Now there are NHL teams in Texas, Florida, and California.

A sport like hockey couldn't grow without innovation, new technology, and new fans. So how did the game get here, and where is it going next? The dawn of indoor arenas and large stadiums had a

The Vegas Golden Knights became the first major professional sports team in Nevada when they debuted in 2017.

big impact on hockey's popularity in the early days, but there were also some key rule changes that helped. The introduction of the forward pass in 1929 may be the most important development in hockey's history. It was once against the rules to make passes to advance the puck. That became very easy to defend, so the NHL decided to change the rule, which opened things up offensively.

The biggest reason to make that change was to promote offense and goal scoring. The league is still trying to find ways to do that today. Sometimes the changes are small, like asking the referees be stricter about the rules and call more penalties. That leads to more power plays, and more power plays usually mean more goals. The NHL has also tried to put limitations on how big the goalies' equipment can be. Goalies are much bigger today than they were in the 1980s when Wayne Gretzky was breaking all kinds of scoring records.

Safety is another area in which the league is constantly innovating and evolving. That usually happens a little more slowly, though. Goalies didn't wear masks for the first 40 years of the NHL, after all. Now you see that every goalie is heavily padded, and every single player on the ice wears a helmet.

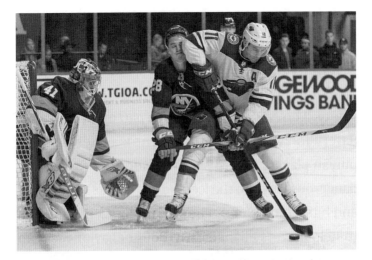

With collisions a part of the game, hockey equipment is always improving to keep players safer.

The rule to make helmets mandatory didn't come in until 1979, and that was only for new players entering the league. Craig MacTavish was the NHL's last player allowed to play without a helmet. He retired in 1997. In 2013, the NHL took things a step further when it also made visors on helmets mandatory to better protect players' eyes.

There have been other inventions in hockey to keep players safer as well. Since players are skating on very sharp pieces of steel, cuts can happen fairly easily. There are new pieces of equipment such as cut-resistant socks and fabrics that players wear to protect themselves from the blades on their opponents' feet. Some players also wear neck guards to protect themselves from skates coming up high.

Equipment isn't the only thing that promotes safety. The NHL formed the Department of Player Safety in 2011. That department was designed to punish players with suspensions or fines for making dangerous plays on the ice, such as checks to the head and hits from behind. The goal of that department is to help players change dangerous behavior that can put their opponents at risk.

When it comes to rules and regulations, the league has continually expanded the role of technology in helping make the right calls on the ice. Video replay review was officially introduced in the NHL in 1991. Back then it was used only to review goals, making sure the puck fully crossed the goal line and that it hadn't been kicked in or bounced off an official on its way into the net. Now, the league uses extensive video review, including offside and goalie interference reviews. The NHL has an office in Toronto called "The Situation Room" where all plays get reviewed to make sure the referees get it right.

As important as on-ice innovations are, there are also many important developments off the ice that help the game grow. A lot of the NHL's popularity is tied to how it reaches fans on television. Making the game more accessible to a bigger audience is always a goal for the league and its broadcast partners.

For example, before the dawn of high-definition TVs, the producers at FOX Sports had an idea of making the puck easier to see on TV. Using the newest technology at the time, FOX had pucks made with computer chips and sensors that allowed them to do something pretty interesting. Fans could more easily see the puck because when it showed up on the broadcast, the puck was glowing. When a player took a hard shot, the glowing puck had a tail behind it. It was called FoxTrax, but fans called it simply the "glow puck."

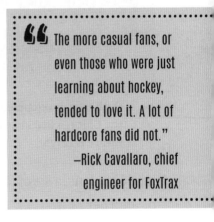

"The more casual fans, or even those who were just learning about hockey, tended to love it," Rick Cavallaro, the chief engineer and project manager of FoxTrax, told *The Hockey News*. "A lot of hardcore fans did not. But even among

> "The more casual fans, or even those who were just learning about hockey, tended to love it. A lot of hardcore fans did not."
> —Rick Cavallaro, chief engineer for FoxTrax

 With new development and exciting players such as the Chicago Blackhawks' Patrick Kane (right), the NHL's future is bright.

hardcore fans, a lot of them seemed to like one aspect or another of it."

FoxTrax lasted only two seasons. It turned out the special pucks were really expensive to make. As can happen many times in a game, pucks leave the ice surface and go into the stands.

The glow puck might not have lasted, but there have been other advancements in TV broadcasts. There have been things like mounting small cameras on referees' helmets, which the NHL has done for some bigger events like the Winter Classic and All-Star Games, to give fans a new perspective on the game.

The league continues to evolve as technology does. There's no telling where it will take the game next.

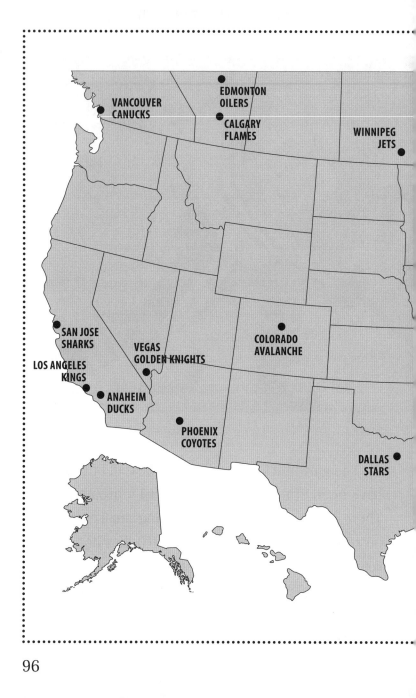

EDMONTON
OILERS

VANCOUVER
CANUCKS

CALGARY
FLAMES

WINNIPEG
JETS

SAN JOSE
SHARKS

VEGAS
GOLDEN KNIGHTS

COLORADO
AVALANCHE

LOS ANGELES
KINGS

ANAHEIM
DUCKS

PHOENIX
COYOTES

DALLAS
STARS

NATIONAL HOCKEY LEAGUE MAP

MINNESOTA
WILD

OTTAWA
SENATORS

MONTREAL
CANADIANS

TORONTO
MAPLE LEAFS

BUFFALO
SABRES

BOSTON
BRUINS

DETROIT
RED WINGS

CHICAGO
BLACKHAWKS

PITTSBURGH
PENGUINS

PHILADELPHIA
FLYERS

NEW YORK ISLANDERS

NEW YORK RANGERS

NEW JERSEY
DEVILS

COLUMBUS
BLUE JACKETS

ST. LOUIS
BLUES

WASHINGTON
CAPITALS

NASHVILLE
PREDATORS

CAROLINA
HURRICANES

TAMPA BAY
LIGHTNING

FLORIDA
PANTHERS

TIMELINE

1875

The first organized indoor hockey game is played in Montreal.

1893

The Montreal AAA win the first Dominion Challenge Trophy, now known as the Stanley Cup.

1909

The Montreal Canadiens are founded and join the National Hockey Association.

1916

The Canadiens win their first of 24 Stanley Cups.

1917

Owners from four professional hockey teams meet at the Windsor Hotel in Montreal and agree to form the National Hockey League.

1926

The Western Canada Hockey League ceases operations, making the NHL the last professional league standing.

1942

The NHL is down to six teams following the tough years of the Great Depression and the start of World War II. The six become known forever as the "Original Six."

1946

Gordie Howe signs with the Detroit Red Wings. His career goes on to touch five decades, and he retires in 1980 as the NHL's all-time leading scorer.

1956

The Canadiens win the first of five Stanley Cups in a row, a run of dominance that remains unmatched in NHL history.

1967

The Original Six era comes to a close when the NHL expands for the first time since the 1940s. The league doubles in size, adding teams in Los Angeles, Minneapolis, Oakland, Philadelphia, Pittsburgh, and St. Louis.

1972

For the first time in decades, the NHL has a true rival when the World Hockey Association is founded. Twelve teams take part in that initial season, with the New England Whalers beating the Winnipeg Jets for the league championship.

1979

The NHL adds four teams from the defunct WHA, bringing Wayne Gretzky to the league. He will go on to become the league's all-time leading scorer.

1988

After four Stanley Cups in five years, the Edmonton Oilers trade Wayne Gretzky to the Los Angeles Kings. The trade is viewed as a groundbreaking moment for the league.

1991

Building upon a new wave of popularity, the NHL adds the San Jose Sharks. By the end of the decade the league adds six more teams.

2000

The NHL completes another round of expansion, adding the Minnesota Wild and the Columbus Blue Jackets, to bring the league to 30 teams.

2003

The Heritage Classic between the Edmonton Oilers and the Montreal Canadiens is the NHL's first outdoor game.

2008

The first Winter Classic is played in Buffalo, New York. Sidney Crosby leads the Pittsburgh Penguins to victory over the host Sabres.

2015

In one of the most anticipated NHL Entry Drafts, the Oilers select Connor McDavid first overall while the Sabres take Jack Eichel second.

2017

The Vegas Golden Knights debut, bringing the NHL to 31 teams and adding another warm-weather city to the growing league.

THE WINNERS

MONTREAL CANADIENS (24 Stanley Cups)

Their first Stanley Cup came in 1916, and they kept on winning. Highlighted by a run of five straight Cups between 1956 and 1960, the Habs have had multiple periods of dominance. However, a long drought began after the team won the 1993 Stanley Cup.

TORONTO MAPLE LEAFS (13)

They have not won the Stanley Cup since the league expanded in 1967, but Toronto's team was quite prolific during the Original Six era. They won four Cups in five years between 1945 and 1949 to become the NHL's first true dynasty.

DETROIT RED WINGS (11)

The Red Wings won their first Stanley Cup in 1936 and had a great run led by Gordie Howe during the 1950s before a long drought set in. That drought ended as the Wings won back-to-back titles in 1997 and 1998. Detroit also took home the Cup in 2002 and 2008.

BOSTON BRUINS (6)

The first American-based team in the NHL, the Bruins got an early start, winning their first Cup in 1929. Things really took off when Bobby Orr arrived as he

helped end a 39-year drought while leading Boston to titles in 1970 and 1972. Most recently, the Bruins won in 2011.

CHICAGO BLACKHAWKS (6)

Winning championships consistently wasn't Chicago's forte until a tremendous run of three Stanley Cups between 2010 and 2015 led by Jonathan Toews and Patrick Kane.

Accurate through the 2017–18 season.

THE BIG THREE

A collection of top performers in various statistics.

MOST CAREER POINTS

1. Wayne Gretzky: 2,857
2. Jaromir Jagr: 1,921
3. Mark Messier: 1,887

MOST CAREER GOALS

1. Wayne Gretzky: 894
2. Gordie Howe: 801
3. Jaromir Jagr: 766

MOST CAREER ASSISTS

1. Wayne Gretzky: 1,963
2. Ron Francis: 1,249
3. Mark Messier: 1,193

HIGHEST CAREER PLUS-MINUS

1. Larry Robinson: 730
2. Bobby Orr: 597
3. Ray Bourque: 528

MOST CAREER HAT TRICKS

1. Wayne Gretzky: 50
2. Mario Lemieux: 40
3. Mike Bossy: 39

MOST CAREER WINS (Goalie)

1. Martin Brodeur: 691
2. Patrick Roy: 551
3. Ed Belfour: 484

MOST CAREER SHUTOUTS (Goalie)

1. Martin Brodeur: 125
2. Terry Sawchuk: 103
3. George Hainsworth: 94

MOST CAREER STANLEY CUPS (Player)

1. Henri Richard: 11

2T. Jean Beliveau: 10

2T. Yvan Cournoyer: 10

Accurate through the 2017–18 season.

FOR MORE INFORMATION

BOOKS

Editors of Sports Illustrated. *Sports Illustrated: The Hockey Book*. New York: Sports Illustrated, 2010.

Gretzky, Wayne, and Kirstie McLellan Day. *99: Stories of the Game*. New York: G. P. Putnam's Sons, 2016.

Peters, Chris. *The Stanley Cup Finals*. Minneapolis: Abdo Publishing, 2013.

ON THE WEB

Elite Prospects
www.eliteprospects.com

Hockey Hall of Fame
www.hhof.com

The Hockey News
www.thehockeynews.com

NHL Statistics resource
www.hockey-reference.com

Official NHL website
www.nhl.com

PLACES TO VISIT

HOCKEY HALL OF FAME

30 Yonge St.
Toronto, ON M5E 1X8
416-360-7765
www.hhof.com

The Hockey Hall of Fame is a comprehensive museum that celebrates the history of the game at the NHL level and beyond. Filled with artifacts and information, it's a mecca for hockey fans.

US HOCKEY HALL OF FAME

801 Hat Trick Ave.
Eveleth, MN 55734
800-443-7825
www.ushockeyhalloffame.com

A shrine to the history of hockey in the United States, the US Hockey Hall of Fame has many artifacts from the past. Additionally, the Hall's "Great Wall of Fame" celebrates the players and other individuals who made the game grow in the United States.

SELECT BIBLIOGRAPHY

BOOKS

Duff, Bob, and Ryan Dixon. *The NHL: 100 Years in Pictures & Stories*. Richmond Hill, ON: Firefly Books, 2016.

Gretzky, Wayne, with Kirstie McLellan Day. *99: Stories of the Game*. New York: G. P. Putnam's Sons, 2016.

Jenish, D'Arcy. *The Montreal Canadiens: 100 Years of Glory*. Toronto: Anchor Canada, 2009.

McKinley, Michael. *Putting a Roof on Winter: Hockey's Rise from Sport to Spectacle*. New York: Greystone, 2000.

ONLINE

Burnside, Scott. "Messier the Finest Leader the Game Has Ever Known." ESPN.com. 15 Sept. 2005. http://www.espn.com/nhl/columns/story?id=2159766. Accessed 1 Mar. 2018.

Higgins, Matt. "Winter Wonderland for Crosby and N.H.L." *New York Times*. 2 Jan. 2008. http://www.nytimes.com/2008/01/02/sports/hockey/02hockey.html. Accessed 1 Mar. 2018.

74shawn. "Joe Sakic Hands Ray Bourque the Stanley Cup 2001 ESPN." *YouTube*. 3 Nov. 2014. www.youtube.com/watch?v=uYHKUNV0FXs&t. Accessed 1 Mar. 2018.

Whyno, Steven. "Wayne Gretzky Trade Brought Credibility to the NHL: Gary Bettman." *Canadian Press*. 8 Aug. 2013. https://www.thestar.com/sports/hockey/2013/08/08/wayne_gretzky_trade_brought_credibility_to_nhl_gary_bettman.html. Accessed 1 Mar. 2018.

INDEX

ABOUT THE AUTHOR

Chris Peters caught the hockey bug while growing up on Chicago's South Side and traveling from rink to rink with his dad to watch the Chicago Blackhawks. He played the sport throughout his youth and managed to turn his passion for the game into a career, not as a player but as a writer. Peters has written for numerous publications and websites and has published three other books on hockey. He currently covers the NHL, the NHL Draft, and hockey prospects across the globe for ESPN. Peters resides in North Liberty, Iowa, with his wife and two children.